Gunman on Campus

Bully on Campus & Online

Drugs & Alcohol

Gunman on Campus

Natural Disasters

Navigating Cyberspace

Peer Pressure & Relationships

Protecting Your Body: Germs, Superbugs, Poison, & Deadly Diseases

Road Safety

Sports

Stranger Danger

Terrorism & Perceived Terrorism Threats

Gunman on Campus

Kim Etingoff

Mason Crest

Mason Crest
450 Parkway Drive, Suite D
Broomall, PA 19008
www.masoncrest.com

Printed and bound in the United States of America.

First printing
9 8 7 6 5 4 3 2 1

Series ISBN: 978-1-4222-3044-2
ISBN: 978-1-4222-3047-3
ebook ISBN: 978-1-4222-8831-3

Library of Congress Cataloging-in-Publication Data

Etingoff, Kim.
  Gunman on campus / Kim Etingoff.
     pages cm. — (Safety first)
  Includes index.
  Audience: Age 10+
  Audience: Grade 4 to 6.
  ISBN 978-1-4222-3044-2 (series) — ISBN 978-1-4222-3047-3 (hardback) — ISBN 978-1-4222-8831-3 (ebook) 1. School shootings—Juvenile literature. 2. School shootings—Prevention—Juvenile literature. 3. School violence—Juvenile literature. 4. School violence—Prevention—Juvenile literature. I. Title.
  LB3013.3.E87 2015
  371.7'82—dc23
                              2014003848

Contents

Introduction   6

1. Real-Life Stories   9

2. What Makes a Gunman
   on Campus Dangerous?   17

3. Staying Safe and Being Prepared   25

4. What Can You Do to Stay Safe?   33

Find Out More   46

Index   47

About the Author & Consultant
   and Picture Credits   48

Introduction

No task is more important than creating safe schools for all children. It should not require an act of courage for parents to send their children to school nor for children to come to school. As adults, we must do everything reasonable to provide a school climate that is safe, secure, and welcoming—an environment where learning can flourish. The educational effectiveness and the strength of any nation is dependent upon a strong and effective educational system that empowers and prepares young people for meaningful and purposeful lives that will promote economic competitiveness, national defense, and quality of life.

Clearly adults are charged with the vital responsibility of creating a positive educational climate. However, the success of young people is also affected by their own participation. The purpose of this series of books is to articulate what young adults can do to ensure their own safety, while at the same time educating them as to the steps that educators, parents, and communities are taking to create and maintain safe schools. Each book in the series gives young people tools that will empower them as participants in this process. The result is a model where students have the information they need to work alongside parents, educators, and community leaders to tackle the safety challenges that face young people every day.

Perhaps one of the most enduring and yet underrated challenges facing young adults is bullying. Ask parents if they can remember the schoolyard bully from when they were in school, and the answers are quite revealing. Unfortunately, the situation is no better today—and new venues for bullying exist in the twenty-first-century world that never existed before. A single bully can intimidate not only a single student but an entire classroom, an entire school, and even an entire community. The problem is underscored by research from the National School Safety Center and the United States Secret Service that indicates that bullying was involved in 80 percent of school shootings over the past two decades. The title in this series that addresses this problem is a valuable and essential tool for promoting safety and stopping bullying.

Another problem that has been highlighted by the media is the threat of violence on our school campuses. In reality, research tells us that schools are the safest place for young people to be. After an incident like Columbine or Sandy Hook, however, it is difficult for the public, including students, to understand that a youngster is a hundred times more likely to be assaulted or killed at home or in the community than at school. Students cannot help but absorb the fears that are so prevalent in our society. Therefore, a frank, realistic, discussion of this topic, one that avoids hysteria and exaggeration, is essential for our young people. This series offers a title on this topic that does exactly that. It addresses questions such as: How do you deal with a gunman on the campus? Should you run, hide, or confront? We do not want to scare our children; instead, we want to empower them and reassure them as we prepare them for such a crisis. The book also covers the changing laws and school policies that are being put in place to ensure that students are even safer from the threat of violence in the school.

"Stranger danger" is another safety threat that receives a great deal of attention in the modern world. Again, the goal should be to empower rather than terrify our children. The book in this series focusing on this topic provides young readers with the essential information that will help them be "safety smart," not only at school but also between home and school, at play, and even when they are home alone.

Alcohol and drug abuse is another danger that looms over our young people. As many as 10 percent of American high school students are alcoholics. Meanwhile, when one student was asked, "Is there a drug problem in your school?" her reply was, "No, I can get all the drugs I want." A book in this series focuses on this topic, giving young readers the information they need to truly comprehend that drugs and alcohol are major threats to their safety and well-being.

From peer pressure to natural disasters, from road dangers to sports safety, the Safety First series covers a wide range of other modern concerns. Keeping children and our schools safe is not an isolated challenge. It will require all of us working together to create a climate where young people can have safe access to the educational opportunities that will promote the success of all children as they transition into becoming responsible citizens. This series is an essential tool for classrooms, libraries, guidance counselors, and community centers as they face this challenge.

Dr. Ronald Stephens
Executive Director
National School Safety Center
www.schoolsafety.us

Words to Know

media: Means of mass communication, including television, the radio, magazines, newspapers, and the Internet.

traumatized: Shocked and emotionally shaken for a long period of time due to an upsetting event.

Chapter One

Real-Life Stories

On April 20, 1999, at Columbine High School near Denver, Colorado, two students pulled out guns and began shooting. When they were done, fifteen students were dead, including the shooters themselves, as well as a teacher. Twenty-three others were wounded. Afterward, the nation reeled in shock and sorrow. People tried to make sense of something that seemed too horrible to be possible. The struggle to put their worlds back together was even harder for Columbine's survivors, the students who had lived through the terrible events. Governments, citizens, and school districts tried to think of ways to make their schools safer.

But school violence didn't end. On March 21, 2005, in Red Lake, Minnesota, a sixteen-year-old killed his grandfather and girlfriend, and then, armed with several guns, went to the Red Lake High School. There, he passed through the metal detector, shot the unarmed school police officer, and went on a ten-minute shooting rampage in the halls of the school. When he ended it by shooting himself, he had killed an English teacher and five students and had left seven wounded. In the investigation that followed, police learned that other students were involved in planning the attack, and a number of other students knew something was going to happen.

Then, on December 14, 2012, a twenty-year-old named Adam Lanza went into Sandy Hook Elementary School in Connecticut, where he shot and killed twenty children and six adult staff

Flowers were left outside this school building in Moscow, Russia, after a teenager described as a model student shot a teacher and a police officer dead, then took more than 20 of his schoolmates hostage in February 2014.

Gunman on Campus

Not Just a Modern Phenomenon

People often assume that school violence is a product of our modern world. But the deadliest incidence of school violence actually took place more than 80 years ago. The Bath School disaster is the name given to three bombings in Bath Township, Michigan, on May 18, 1927, an event that killed forty-five people and injured fifty-eight, most of them children in the second to sixth grades. The bomber was a school board member, Andrew Kehoe, who was upset by a property tax town members had to pay to fund the construction of the school building. He blamed the tax for his own financial hardships. He had been secretly planting explosives in the school building for many months.

members. As police officer and emergency workers arrived, he committed suicide by shooting himself in the head. It was one of deadliest mass shootings in America's history.

School shootings have gotten a lot of attention lately. Several years earlier, a rash of school shootings occurred in places such as Moses Lake, Washington; Bethel, Alaska; Pearl, Mississippi; West Paducah, Kentucky; Jonesboro, Arkansas; Springfield, Oregon; and Columbine High School in Littleton, Colorado. And the problem wasn't confined to schools in the United States. There were also fatal episodes in schools in Scotland, Yemen, the Netherlands, Germany, and Sweden. Canadian schools had not had a fatal school shooting in twenty years, but on April 18, 1999, just eight days after the Columbine incident, a youth entered a high school in Taber, Alberta, and killed one student and seriously wounded another.

The horrifying news stories of senseless shootings in schools have given the impression that schools are a dangerous place to be—but actually school violence has not increased. Instead, a report issued in 2004 indicated that violent crime against students actually fell by 50 percent in the previous ten years. The coverage from news **media** makes us feel as though this is terrible and growing problem. It isn't a growing problem, but it is terrible: even one school shooting is too much! Students in today's schools don't always feel safe.

A SURVIVOR'S STORY

When Marjorie Lindholm woke up on the morning of the Columbine shootings, she was thinking about a boy. She wasn't expecting anything out of the ordinary from the day, nothing more exciting than having a chance to talk to him. Marjorie was a sophomore who had just made the cheerleading squad; she was hoping to go on to become a doctor when she was older. Her plans for the future were made, her life on course. She certainly wasn't expecting that later that afternoon, two students at her school would kill thirteen people. And she had no way of knowing how that would change her own life as well.

As Marjorie sat in her fifth-period class, taking a biology test, she heard something that sounded like rocks against a window. Her teacher told the class it was probably some sort of senior prank.

Real-Life Stories

Witnessing the deaths of your classmates is an awful experience—many teens who go through such an ordeal need to talk it over it with a counselor or therapist afterward.

"But, then," Marjorie told a reporter, "we heard screaming so horrible you'd never want to hear it again."

For the next four hours, Marjorie crouched in the classroom, listening to the turmoil in the rest of the building. Fire alarms blared. Her favorite teacher, Coach Sanders, died in the same room with her after being shot twice. "Dead bodies don't look like they do in the movies," Marjorie realized.

She told a reporter from WebMD, "I think with Columbine, people don't really realize, [the degree of emotional trauma depends on] kind of where you were at the school. If somebody was at the far end of it and ran out of the school right away, I don't think they were as **traumatized** as someone who was stuck in the library or the science room or saw someone shot. So I think there were lots of different levels of trauma that occurred with Columbine."

Gunman on Campus

Until the terrible events in 1999, Columbine High School was just an ordinary school like any other.

For months after the violence, Marjorie had stomachaches and nightmares. She got sick with fevers again and again. Eventually, a month into her senior year, she dropped out of school. Sitting in a classroom was something she could no longer handle. She earned her GED (a set of tests that show you have learned as much as you would have if you had a high school diploma), but then she faced the same difficulties when she tried to attend college: classrooms had become terrifying places for her. Her life had veered off track in a way she could never have known would happen— and she had no idea how to get it back on course.

"I didn't even deal with it for years," Marjorie told a reporter. "It just wasn't spoken about."

Her mother, a professional counselor, suggested that Marjorie start keeping a journal to help her confront her emotions and thoughts. That journal turned into a book: *A Columbine Survivor's Story.*

This memorial at Columbine High School is a reminder that although communities and individuals eventually heal after a school shooting, the tragedy can never be forgotten.

You might say that the violence in Columbine High School destroyed many lives, including Marjorie's, in addition to the fifteen people who actually died. But despite her struggles, Marjorie believes she has come out of this a better person and strives to make the most of her life. She switched to an online course of college study, and she tries to move ahead with her life, even though it's a different life than the one she'd once planned.

Marjorie hopes her book will help young people deal with their own traumas or hardships. "(The shootings) put in perspective the things I really care about," she said. "I feel more prepared for things now. Nothing can be worse than what I've faced."

Every time another school shooting happens, Marjorie reaches out to the survivors.

THE OUTSIDERS' HEROES

After Columbine, people were scared . . . angry . . . sad. Some people hated the shooters. Others felt that that the shooters were victims as much as the others who died that day. And still others admired Eric Harris and Dylan Klebold, the two young men responsible for the violence at Columbine.

For some young people, Eric and Dylan were symbols with whom they could identify. They were outsiders, kids who had had enough of being ignored, harassed, and bullied. They'd finally gotten angry and taken action. The ability to shake a nation is tremendous power for a young

Factors That May Have Contributed to the Shooters' Actions

In the months after Columbine, many experts searched for the reasons behind Eric and Dylan's violence. They put forward several possible factors:

- high school cliques that excluded Eric and Dylan
- a climate of bullying that the Columbine school allowed
- the influence of violent video games
- the influence of heavy-metal lyrics

Ultimately, however, these are only theories. Eric and Dylan committed suicide after the shootings, so no one can ask them their reasons.

person who has felt ignored and insignificant for most of his life. Eric and Dylan may be dead—but in some kids' minds, they went out in a blaze of glory. The media's obsession with school violence feeds into this.

This reaction scares people like Marjorie. She knows that violence is never, ever the answer, no matter how angry and hurt you are. Marjorie recommends that instead people fight back against the imaginary boundaries that separate us. "I know there [are] cliques and there always will be," she said, "but if [people] could just be accepting for right now and make sure nobody's alone, even the weird kid that sits in the corner. You know, you have to watch out for everyone right now."

Incidents of school violence ask us to change ourselves. We need to examine who we are. Do we categorize people, set up boundary lines that include some people while they shut others out? Is there something inside us, in the way our friends and we act, or in the things we allow to go on around us that could contribute to a Columbine in our community?

No one should feel afraid when they go to school. So what steps can we take to make sure every student feels safe?

Words to Know

gang violence: Fights between groups of criminals, sometimes with weapons such as guns.

witness: See or hear, usually used to talk about seeing or hearing something related to a crime.

anxious: Very worried or nervous, sometimes without a specific reason.

urban: In a city or to do with cities.

Chapter Two

What Makes a Gunman on Campus Dangerous?

People with guns on a school campus are dangerous for obvious reasons. They can hurt or kill students and school workers. But just how dangerous are they?

THE FACTS

School shootings are pretty rare, but when they do occur, and they are scary. But you don't have to be scared they'll happen to you. It is very unlikely you'll ever be a part of a school shooting.

For example, during the 2009–2010 school year, seventeen students were killed at school (most by guns). But there were fifty-five million students going to school during the same period. Of course, even seventeen is too high a number. But it is still a very small number when you think of the millions of students going to school.

Think about it this way. Twice as many young people die in car accidents than by guns every year. And only a very small percentage of those who are killed by guns are killed at school. Only one in one hundred of all the kids killed by guns are killed at school. That's not very many!

A school shooting can affect many people, not just the ones who are shot. Here, volunteers hold a candle vigil to remember the terrible events of the Sandy Hook Elementary shooting.

Gunman on Campus

Some Gun Facts

Here are some facts about guns in the United States, from DoSomething.org:

- Civilians (non-police) own 270 million guns. The police have 897,000.
- Factories made 5.5 million new guns in the United States in 2010.
- About 33,000 people in the United States died because of guns in 2011.
- An average of 268 people are shot every day in the United States, though not all of them die.
- Only nine states have laws that make people have trigger locks on their guns.
- Since 1950, almost every public shooting of multiple people happened somewhere that had banned people from carrying guns.

Most school shootings involve only one person with a gun and one victim. School shootings like the ones at Columbine and Sandy Hook Elementary School are even more rare.

When school shootings happen, they make the news. It can make it seem like they happen all the time. But they happen at very few schools each year.

Youth violence in schools is actually falling. Shootings are just one form of violence at school. Other types of violence, like **gang violence**, make schools dangerous. Fewer young people belong to gangs across the country, and fewer students bring weapons to school. We still have a long way to go to end violence in schools. But we're headed in the right direction.

WITNESSES

Gunmen on campuses are dangerous because they can hurt and kill people. But they can also hurt people they don't physically injure.

Think back to Marjorie's story. She wasn't shot. But she was still deeply affected by what happened. She knew the victims. Her community was ripped apart. The shooting had a big effect on the rest of her life.

The same is true for lots of other young people who **witness** school shootings or who were close to them. They are injured emotionally.

Witnesses of shootings might be scared all the time. They might be angry. They might even become violent themselves. Like Sarah, many need therapy to learn how to deal with the shooting.

Witnesses can include students in the school who weren't hurt. They include the police, firefighters, and ambulance workers who arrive at the school to help. Victims' families are deeply hurt. A lot of people get hurt in a school shooting.

President Obama pauses during a meeting to observe a moment of silence in the Oval Office to remember the 20 children and six adults killed in the Sandy Hook Elementary School shooting in Newtown, Connecticut.

Gunman on Campus

Guns and Video Games

People like to argue about whether violent video games lead to real-life violence. On one side, people say that violent games make guns and shooting normal. They teach gamers how to shoot and make using a gun more like a game. Some scientists think this is true. Other people think the link between violent video games and violence isn't so simple. Not much scientific research proves the link. And overall, violence in the United States is falling. Scary violence, like school shootings, is often featured on the news. But there are actually fewer violent crimes than there used to be, even though more people are playing violent video games. Nobody knows for sure how much violent video games have to do with real-life violence.

FEAR

Even if there has never been someone with a gun at your school, you might still be scared it could happen. Hearing or reading about school shootings in the news doesn't help. You may start to think it could happen to you.

School should be a safe place, not somewhere you're scared to be. Some people react really strongly to news of school shootings. Kids in the community where a shooting takes place will need help coping with their fear. But young people at schools far from the shootings can get very upset, too.

If you're scared to go to school, learning gets harder. When you're scared or **anxious**, it's harder to pay attention in class. You might find yourself getting angry at people. Or fake being sick, so you don't have to go to school. You might even make yourself sick by worrying so much. You might have trouble sleeping, so you are too tired to learn in school.

You might start learning less. It may be harder to get along with the teacher or other students. Your grades might start to slip. You don't have to be in the middle of school shootings to feel their effects.

Feeling scared usually gets better with time. The news stops reporting stories about the shooting. Then things can go back to normal.

But for some people, being scared never really goes away. For a long time, it didn't for Sarah. Young people who are extremely worried about a shooter at school should talk to an adult and get help. We'll talk more about how to solve this problem in chapter 4.

BRINGING GUNS TO SCHOOL

Not all school shootings are the same. Shootings that get the most attention are the ones where many people are killed or hurt.

But most school shootings involve one person who brings a gun to school to hurt one particular person. Maybe two people have gotten in a fight. Instead of figuring out how to deal with the fight peacefully, one student brings a gun to school and shoots the other.

In 2006, about 3000 students were expelled from school for bringing a gun onto school grounds. It's important that guns not be in school to create a safe place to learn.

Gunman on Campus

School Shootings Around the World

The most school shootings in the world happen in the United States. They happen way more often in the United States than in other countries. But school shootings do happen from time to time in other countries. In recent years, students have been killed in schools in Canada, Norway, France, Brazil, Germany, Azerbaijan, Scotland, Yemen, and more. School shootings are a worldwide problem.

Every year, some students bring guns to school. In 2005 the Centers for Disease Control and Prevention found that over a million high school students brought a weapon—usually a gun or knife—to school at least once a month. Not all of those students use the guns to kill other students. But a few do. And no one should be bringing weapons to school at all!

Students in schools across the country bring guns to school. But it's most common in **urban** schools. Gun violence is common in some urban neighborhoods. Too many young people die every day from gun violence. They are usually killed on the streets, not in school. But a few every year are killed in schools.

School shootings involving many people haven't happened very often in urban schools. They happen more in rural and suburban schools. Researchers are still trying to figure out why school gun violence happens where it does.

No matter where school violence happens, or how many people are killed or hurt, it has to stop. And lots of people are working toward that goal.

Words to Know

organizations: Groups of people working toward the same goals.
security: Things done to prevent a crime from happening Guards, locks, and alarms are all forms of security.
peer: Someone who is part of the same group as another person.
consistent: Always the same.
expel: To force someone to leave a school, sometimes because of violence or bad behavior.
disorderly conduct: Bad behavior or not following rules.
policies: Spelled-out ways of doing things.

DRUG FREE

GUN FREE
SCHOOL ZONE
VIOLATORS WILL FACE SEVERE
FEDERAL STATE AND LOCAL
CRIMINAL PENALTIES

Chapter Three

Staying Safe and Being Prepared

People know school shootings are a problem. Even though they are rare, one shooter at a school is too many. And many people and **organizations** have set about trying to find solutions.

SCHOOL SECURITY

Many schools think the answer to gun violence is more **security**. More schools have added security as a result of school shootings over the past few years.

Schools lock their doors after classes have started. People have to sign in and wear name tags when they visit. Metal detectors and gates and security cameras are found in many schools. Police officers or guards stand at the doors. Maybe your school already has some of these things.

Even more schools increased security after the Sandy Hook shootings. In one survey given out after the shootings, almost three out of four schools had done something to make their buildings safer.

Lots of schools added new locks or closed doors that were open before. Others added more safety drills, so students and teachers would know what to do in case of an emergency. A few added police officers or asked the police to drive by more often.

25

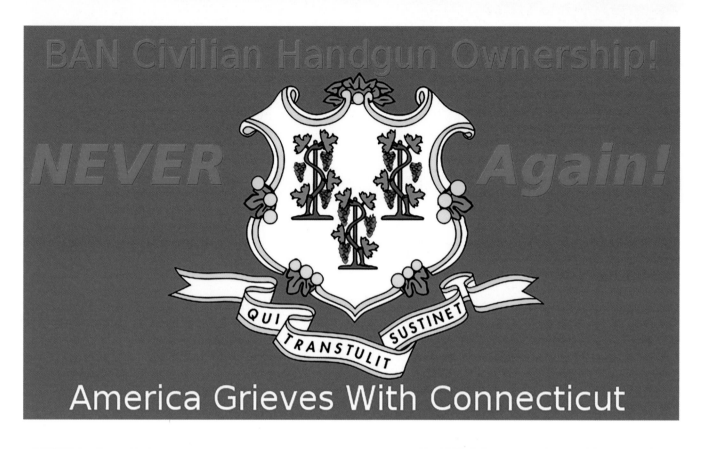

After the shooting at Sandy Hook, groups across the United States spoke out against gun violence with posters like these. The Youth Justice Coalition said they know from experience that the answer to violence in schools is not to put more guns in schools, even if they're in the hands of authorities.

Gunman on Campus

ENDING GUN VIOLENCE

School shootings are part of a bigger problem—gun violence. People with problems should not turn to guns and violence. But, unfortunately, that's what sometimes happens.

One organization in southern California is taking on gun violence. The organization is called Youth Alive! The organization uses some of its programs to help young people end gun violence. The first one is called Teens on Target.

Teens on Target focuses on young people who live in neighborhoods with a lot of crime and gun violence. The twelve-week program trains them to teach others about gun violence. These young people become *peer* educators. They lead classes about stopping violence. They work with other people in the community to stop violence. They encourage their friends to stop carrying guns.

Peer educators are great teachers. Many of them have seen gun violence up close. Some have been shot themselves. They get to share their stories and help stop gun violence. They also get paid, because this is a job!

Another program Youth Alive! has is called Caught in the Crossfire. The program works with young people who have been hurt by violence and are recovering in the hospital.

Intervention specialists work for this program. They are people who have already experienced violence. They come to hospitals to work with young people who have just been hurt by violence themselves.

People from the program continue to help these young people after they leave the hospital. They work with them to feel better about their lives. And they keep them from turning to violence.

Without Caught in the Crossfire, hurt, young people might think about getting revenge. Once they get better, they may want to hurt the person or people who hurt them. Workers in the program help them stay out of trouble and find nonviolent ways to heal.

Youth Alive! lists their values on their website. Their values help them fight against gun violence. For example, they value relentlessness, or never giving up. They say, "Not only will we do what we say we will do, we will not stop until we achieve our goal, no matter the barriers. We are *consistent* in our commitment to provide services from beginning to end."

The organization also values community. "We are of, by, and for the community. We partner with others in the movement so that our work has real life effect at the neighborhood level. We are life-changing!"

And members of Youth Alive! value courage. They state, "We bravely engage in situations where others fear to go, because our community bravely works to change their lives despite the odds against them."

Youth Alive! and programs like it are helping end gun violence in neighborhoods and in schools. If we can end gun violence everywhere, school shootings will hopefully become part of the past.

YOUNG PEOPLE STANDING UP FOR PEACE

The Youth Justice Coalition is a group of mostly young people of color who have grown up around gun violence in California. They fight for the rights of young people to live in a peaceful world.

Many schools are installing metal detectors to increase security—but these measures might not be the best way to create a safe learning environment.

Gunman on Campus

Teenagers who are expelled from school are more likely to get in trouble than those who stay in school.

After the Sandy Hook shooting, the Youth Justice Coalition released a statement with some of its own ideas about how to end gun violence.

The statement said, "As youth growing up on some of America's deadliest streets, we are all too familiar with gun violence and its impacts. Too many of us have been shot and shot at. We have buried our friends and our family members. Nearly all of us have been to more funerals than graduations. No one wants the violence to stop more than we do.

"But, we have also seen how attempts to build public safety with security systems, armed police, and prisons have failed."

The Youth Justice Coalition lists eleven ways people can improve gun violence.

Their first demand is to end zero-tolerance policies in schools. Zero-tolerance means schools suspend or **expel** students who break a rule. Expelling students doesn't help them stay out of trouble, though.

Their second demand is to get rid of rules that expel students who argue with school officials or are accused of "**disorderly conduct**." Again, students who aren't in school don't stay out of trouble.

They go on to reject more police and military at schools. They also reject more security gates, metal detectors, and security cameras. Instead, they say, "Replace school police and school resource officers with intervention/peacebuilders."

Peacebuilders are adults who make school safer. They make it safe to walk to and from school.

Staying Safe and Being Prepared

Turning schools into community centers—facilities that offer many different services to their communities—might be a good way to keep them safer.

Gunman on Campus

More Guns in School?

People can't ever seem to agree about guns, even when it comes to schools. Opponents to guns don't want any in school. They think guns in schools are dangerous—no matter who has them. Gun supporters think schools would be safer if there were more guns in school, as long as the right people have them. They believe more police and guards make schools safer. Some people argue letting teachers bring guns to class is a good idea. That way, if a shooter comes into a classroom, the teacher can protect the students. What do you think?

They work with students who are in trouble and might turn to guns. They run antiviolence programs. They work with young people who are fighting so that they can end their fight without violence.

The statement supports **policies** that help students learn how to deal with problems without violence. The Youth Justice Coalition wants policies that "hold students accountable for our actions in ways that keep us in school, cause self-reflection and growth, and improve our relationships with school staff."

Another demand is to make schools into community centers. Schools would be open all year, every day. Young people could use their school all the time as a safe place. They could get homework help and college prep there. They could be trained for jobs. They could play sports or do art every day. They could even go to the doctor there.

The statement offers lots of suggestions to stop gun violence on the streets and in schools. They include:

- Bringing in jobs to struggling communities where gun violence is common.
- Bringing in peacebuilders to every school.
- Teaching anti-gun programs in schools.
- Treating young people who have post-traumatic stress disorder from violence.
- Having programs where people turn in their guns, without anyone asking them where they got them. People who turn in the guns get money or food.
- Training police officers to work on building peace, not violence.

The statement says, "We are the experts on school and community safety. We need to be at the center of decision-making regarding policy changes that will impact our blocks and our classrooms."

The Youth Justice Coalition hopes to make neighborhoods and schools safe from guns and other violence. Maybe if the people in charge listened, we could make that happen!

Words to Know

paranoid schizophrenia: A type of mental illness that can lead to believing that bad people are out to get you.

psychologists: People who study the mind and emotions.

psychiatrists: Medical doctors who focus on the emotions and mental health.

social workers: People who provide services to help people cope with the challenges in their lives.

compassion: Ability to feel others' pain—and then do something to help.

challenge: Call us to do better than what we've been doing.

stress: When we feel like life is too much to handle. Stress makes it hard for our bodies and emotions to work the way they're supposed to.

researchers: People who look for answers by doing tests and studies.

Chapter Four

What Can You Do to Stay Safe?

When you read about school shootings in the news, it's normal to be scared. Fortunately, you can take steps to be a little less scared. You can also do some things to stop school shootings and help end violence at school.

LEARN THE FACTS

You can be a little less scared about school shootings by learning the facts. Chapter 1 gives you an idea of how often school shootings happen. The facts say school shootings are very rare.

It also helps to understand why school shootings happen. Every shooter turns to violence for a different reason. There are a few trends, though, that help explain school shootings.

Many people who shoot others at school are angry about being bullied or teased. That's absolutely no reason to kill other students. But you can start to see why they were angry. There are better ways of dealing with anger.

School shooters are often lonely. They don't fit in with other students. They may have been bullied and made to feel even worse. They just want the pain to stop. Instead of talking to someone and figuring out how to solve their problems, they turn to violence.

33

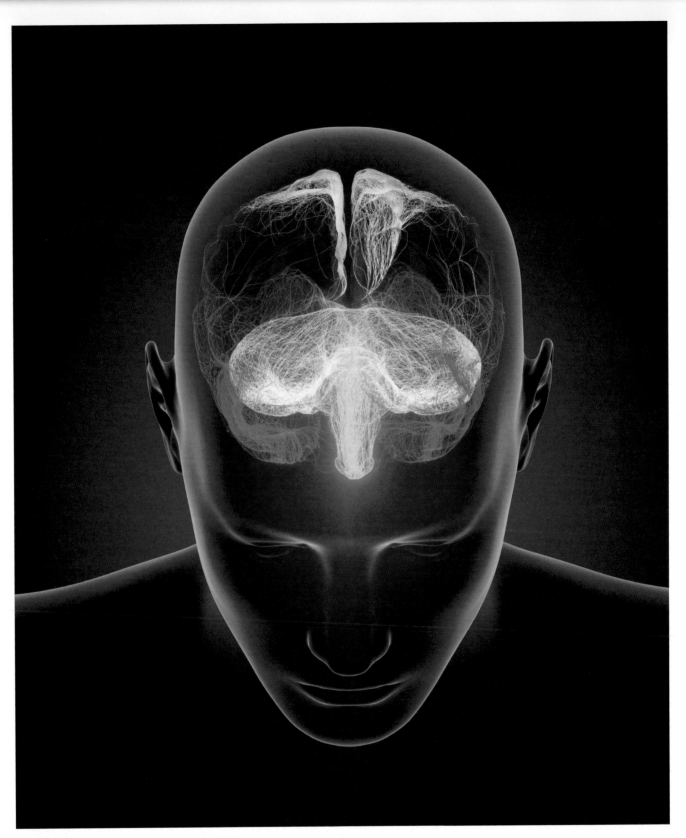

People who are mentally ill are not evil. Instead, their brains don't function correctly, which may make them see and hear things that aren't real. Very few people with mental illness are violent, but when they are, it's usually because they believe they are defending themselves from some danger to themselves.

Gunman on Campus

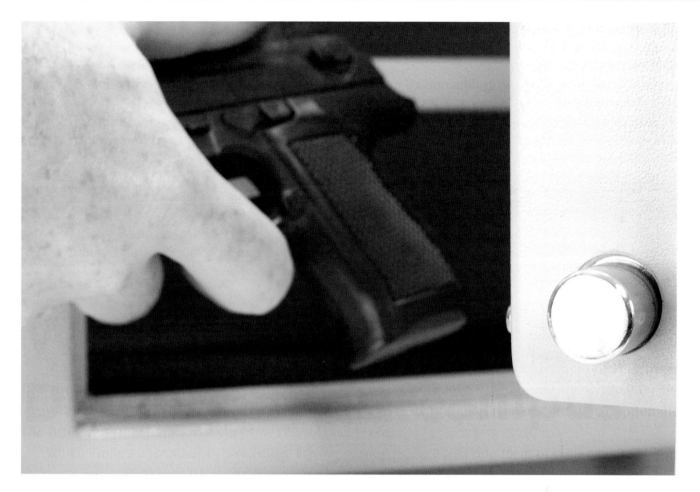

People who own guns should keep them in a safe place, like this gun safe, so they can't be used in dangerous ways.

Other school shooters have a mental illness. The shooter at Sandy Hook was mentally ill. Some therapists who talked with him diagnosed him with **_paranoid schizophrenia_**.

Years before he committed murder at Sandy Hook, the shooter had posted on a website that he believed people were trying to control his mind. He hated holidays, he wrote. He hated bright lights, even sunshine. He couldn't bear loud noises. The world was a terrifying place for him. He was obsessed with violence—and meanwhile, his family had many automatic weapons. The combination was deadly. But no one paid attention to this desperately ill young man, even though he posted his thoughts publically and even told a call-in radio station that he believed mass killings were necessary because the world was so evil.

Not every gunman is mentally ill. But it helps explain why certain people end up as shooters.

Other reasons include easy access to guns. Shooters often bring guns from home. Or they buy them. Some steal them from other people's homes, where they aren't locked up properly.

No matter the reasons, school shootings are obviously never OK. But learning some of the

Telling a police officer or some other adult can prevent school shootings before they happen.

36

Gunman on Campus

reasons behind them can help make shootings easier to understand. Knowing the facts usually helps victims, witnesses, and others deal with the whole thing.

GUN SAFETY

Guns are dangerous weapons. They aren't toys. If you ever come across a gun, stay away from it.

Some people keep guns at home. Some are for hunting. Some are for target practice. Some are for protection.

No matter what the gun is for, leave it alone. If you find a gun in your home, you might want to play with it. That's how accidents happen. You don't know if the gun is loaded or how to use it safely. Playing with guns can injure yourself or anyone around you.

And you should never bring a gun to school. Once in a while, a student brings a gun to school to show off. She thinks it would be cool to have a gun at school, even if she doesn't really plan on using it.

Of course, bringing a gun to school is also really dangerous. You could get in a lot of trouble if someone finds the gun. Don't let that be you. Plus, you could hurt or kill someone accidentally.

SAY SOMETHING

Before most school shootings, the gunman says something to other students. He might say that he's going to bring a gun to school. Or that "something big" is going to happen next week, but he's keeping it a secret. He might even show another student his gun.

School shootings have been stopped because someone said something to an adult. One school shooting in Florida was stopped for that reason. Two boys were planning on shooting lots of people at their school. They even had a list of names.

Someone found out. A friend of one of the would-be shooters showed his or her mom text messages from the shooter and pictures of the shooter with a gun. The friend also knew the shooter wanted to kill himself.

Police met with the two boys. They confessed their plan. They also said they heard voices and wanted to kill themselves. They were sent away to get help.

The school will never know if the boys really would have shot students or school staff. But the student who told was a hero and helped avoid a tragedy.

If you hear someone talking like that, tell an adult right away. You can tell a teacher, guidance counselor, or any other adult who works in the school. If one person doesn't take you seriously, tell another. But the first person you tell will probably take you very seriously.

You don't have to tell somebody in front of all your classmates. You can talk to an adult in private and tell her what you heard. No one will know you passed along the information. And you won't get in trouble.

If you're really uncomfortable talking to an adult at school, tell an adult in your family. Your family member can call the school and tell someone.

Maybe nothing would ever have happened. But you never know. You're better off telling an

What Can You Do to Stay Safe?

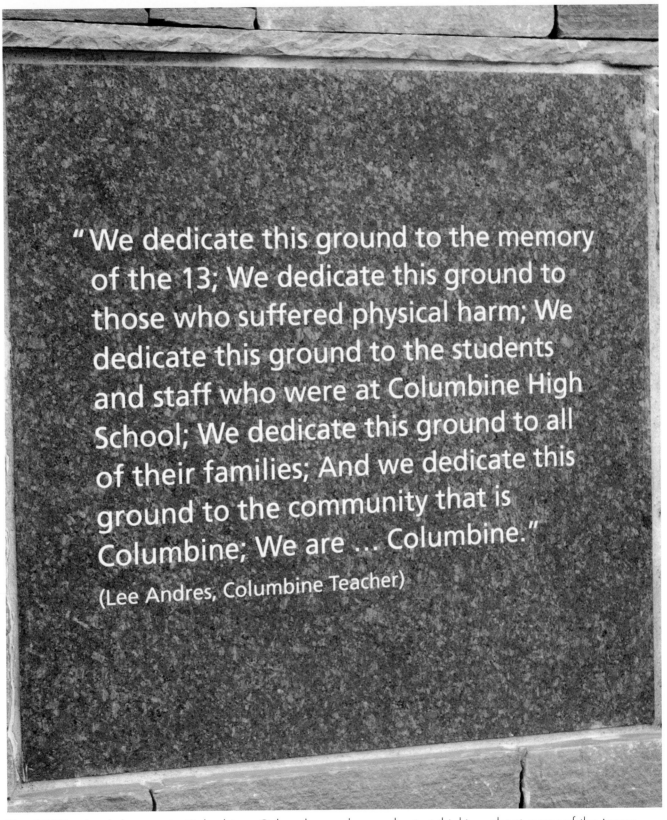

"We dedicate this ground to the memory of the 13; We dedicate this ground to those who suffered physical harm; We dedicate this ground to the students and staff who were at Columbine High School; We dedicate this ground to all of their families; And we dedicate this ground to the community that is Columbine; We are ... Columbine."

(Lee Andres, Columbine Teacher)

The 1999 school shooting in Columbine, Colorado, made people start thinking about many of the issues surrounding guns and safety in schools. This memorial wall is a reminder to the community to never forget.

Gunman on Campus

adult about a potential shooting. The old saying, "It's better to be safe than sorry," is definitely true. By talking, you might be saving lives!

GETTING HELP

Help is available for anything to do with guns and violence should you need it. Many adults are trained to help you deal with your problems.

Talk to someone if you feel upset about school shootings you hear about on the news. No one will think you're strange if you need some help getting past your worries.

And if, like Marjorie, you were close to a school shooting, you should definitely talk to someone. You might not think you're so upset, but you might be burying your feelings.

In either of these situations, there are lots of people you can talk to. Your school probably has a guidance counselor and a school psychologist. Both are trained to help students work through problems.

You can also see a professional therapist outside of school. **Psychologists**, **psychiatrists**, and **social workers** can all help you talk about things that are bothering you. They'll help you figure out why you feel the way you do. And they'll help you find a way to deal with your feelings.

Talk to one of these people if you feel very bad about anything going on in your life. Young people sometimes turn to violence because of serious problems in their lives. They are bullied at school. Or they are having problems at home. Maybe someone close to them has died.

Violence is never the answer to problems. Don't let yourself turn to violence. Talk to someone first!

THE POWER OF FORGIVENESS

On a quiet October morning in Pennsylvania's Lancaster County, a teacher was with her class of Amish students in a one-room schoolhouse. The kids ranged in age from six years old to teenagers. They all looked up when a man came in the building. Many of the children may have recognized him as the man who drove the milk truck that stopped each day at their farms. The man went outside, then came back. This time he carried a handgun in his hand.

The man—whom the world would later learn was Charles Carl Roberts—told the boys in the classroom to help him unload his pickup truck. The teacher took the opportunity to escape and run for help. When Roberts saw her leave, he ordered one of the boys to stop her and threatened to shoot everyone if their teacher got away. The teacher had already reached a nearby farm, however, where she asked the farmer to call 911.

Roberts let some more people go, and one little girl escaped. The boys were still outside. That left ten girls inside with Roberts. He barricaded the front door and ordered the girls to line up against the chalkboard.

A few minutes later the state troopers arrived. Roberts told the troopers he would shoot the girls if they didn't leave. The police officers backed away, but they didn't leave. They talked to Roberts with a loudspeaker. They tried to persuade him to let the girls go.

Amish children, much like those at the school where the shooting took place, walk to school carrying their lunches.

People gathered around the schoolhouse. Then they heard gunshots. The troopers ran to the school. They broke down the door and carried out the girls. Roberts was dead. He had shot himself.

Ambulances rushed to the scene, but three of the girls were already dead. Two more died early the next morning, leaving five more in the hospital. The youngest girl who died was six years old, and the oldest only thirteen.

Roberts, like many other school shooters, was emotionally disturbed. The survivors from the schoolhouse said that before he started shooting, he told them, "I'm angry at God and I need to punish some Christian girls to get even with him. . . . I'm going to make you pay for my daughter." (Roberts had had a baby daughter who died in 1997.) Across the Internet, bloggers described Roberts as "sick," "evil," and "disgusting."

Gunman on Campus

After the shooting at Columbine, friends needed each other more than ever. Here two students hug each other in the aftermath of the shooting.

But the people he had hurt the most, the Amish community, did something surprising: they reached out to Roberts' wife and family. One of the fathers of the dead girls said, "The pain of the killer's parents is ten times my pain. You would just feel terrible if you were the parent of a killer."

The Roberts family was amazed and grateful when Amish community members visited and comforted them. The Amish normally do not mix with others from outside their community, but they reached out now. For nearly an hour, one Amish man held Roberts' sobbing father in his arms, comforting him. They hugged Roberts' widow and other members of his family. They brought food and flowers to the Roberts' home. Of the seventy-five people at the killer's burial, more than half were Amish. Many were parents who had just buried their own children a day or so before. The Amish community also set up a fund to help Roberts' family.

What Can You Do to Stay Safe?

If you're ever in a situation where something scary is going on, look for the people who are helping—police, firefighters, and emergency workers, as well as everyday people who are stepping up to help. These are the people who can help you stay safe.

Gunman on Campus

Who Are the Amish?

The Amish practice a lifestyle that sets them apart from the rest of the modern world. They don't have telephones or electricity in their homes and schools. They don't drive cars and they dress in dark colors. Church and family are at the center of their world. Amish children attend Amish schools, one-room schoolhouses for children in grades one through eight. About 227,000 Amish currently live in the United States, mostly in Pennsylvania, Indiana, Ohio, and New York State. There are also Amish communities in Ontario, Canada.

Marie Roberts, the shooter's wife, wrote a letter to her Amish neighbors, thanking them for their forgiveness: "Your love for our family has helped to provide the healing we so desperately need. . . . Your **compassion** has reached beyond our family, beyond our community, and is changing our world."

Some people criticized the Amish community's attitude. Many people felt that forgiveness made no sense when such terrible evil had been done.

The Amish believe that violence should be prevented. They believe that those that commit violence must face consequences that will prevent future violence. But they also believe that forgiveness is the first step toward a future that is more hopeful.

As a symbol of their attitude toward the violence, the week after the shooting, the Amish tore down the building where it had happened. They built a new schoolhouse, called the New Hope School, in a different spot. They made the new building as different as possible from the old one, so that their kids could go back to school and feel safe.

WHAT'S THE ANSWER?

The shooting at Nickel Mines schoolhouse was the third school shooting in less than a week. Earlier that week, a gunman had killed a student and then shot himself at Platte Canyon High School in Bailey, Colorado. Two days later, at Weston High School in Wisconsin, a student had shot and killed the principal. Nickel Mines was the twenty-fourth school shooting in the United States in 2006. People were upset.

President George W. Bush held a conference to discuss school violence. School districts across the country—and around the world—tried to understand the problem. New programs were started, new laws were passed, and communities worked together. And then more school shootings happened.

Remember, though, school shootings are still very rare. But even one shooting in a school is too much. After the shooting at Sandy Hook, many Americans, including President Obama, called for stricter gun laws. They said that if angry and mentally ill people couldn't get guns so easily, fewer shootings would happen. But other Americans disagreed. "The only thing that stops a bad guy with a gun is a good guy with a gun," said the vice president of the National Rifle Association.

You can help build safe schools by respecting others' differences and building friendships.

44

Gunman on Campus

While people argued over this issue, though, schools and communities were doing everything else they could to keep schools safe.

The way that the Amish handled a school shooting is a **challenge** to all of us. It's too easy to hate people who do bad things. Psychologists, however, say that the Amish community's forgiveness is far healthier, both for themselves and for the entire world.

It turns out that forgiveness reduces **stress**. Holding on to fear and anger makes you more likely to get sick. You can't remember as well when you're scared and angry, and you can't learn as well. People who can forgive are also able to build closer friendships. But people who hold grudges often become loners. **Researchers** have found that people who have close connections to others are safer in lots of ways. They can work together to protect themselves from violence—and they don't spread violence themselves.

Violence creates vicious circles. The kids who are bullied sometimes turn around and become killers. This can make students less accepting of other kids who are different—and the cycle continues.

You don't have to be scared, though! Countries, communities, and schools are working hard to protect students. And you can do your part. Pay attention. If you hear someone who sounds upset and angry, tell an adult. Meanwhile, help build a world where violence no longer seems like a good answer to anyone.

Find Out More

ONLINE

Cause: Bullying and Violence
www.dosomething.org/issues/school-violence

Gun Safety
kidshealth.org/kid/watch/er/gun_safety.html

Should You Worry about School Violence?
kidshealth.org/teen/school_jobs/bullying/school_violence.html#cat20181

Statement by Youth of Color on School Safety and Gun Violence in America
www.youth4justice.org/wp-content/uploads/2013/04/04-01-13YouthofColorResponsetoSchool-ShootingsFinalStatement.pdf

Stopping School Violence
www.ncpc.org/resources/files/pdf/school-safety/stopping_school_violence.pdf

IN BOOKS

Becnel, Barbara C., and Stanley Tookie Williams. *Gangs and Weapons*. New York: Powerkids Press, 2003.

Cruz, Barbara. *School Shootings and School Violence: A Hot Issue*. Berkeley Heights, N.J.: Enslow Publications, 2002.

Drew, Naomi. *The Kids' Guide to Working Out Conflicts: How to Keep Cool, Stay Safe, and Get Along*. Minneapolis, Minn.: Free Spirit Publishing, 2004.

Gimpel, Diane Marczely. *Violence in Video Games*. Minneapolis, Minn.: Core Library, 2013.

Hasday, Judy L. *Forty-Nine Minutes of Madness: The Columbine High School Shooting*. Berkeley Heights, N.J.: Enslow Publications, 2012.

Index

adults 9, 20–21, 29, 36–37, 39, 45
Amish 39–41, 43, 45

bullying 15, 46

Caught in the Crossfire 27
Columbine High School 9, 11–15, 19, 38, 41

elementary school 9, 19–20

facts 17, 19, 33, 37
firefighters 19, 42

gangs 16, 19
guidance counselor 37, 39
guns 9, 16–17, 19, 21–23, 25–27, 29, 31, 35,
   37–39, 43
gun safety 37

high school 9, 11, 13–15, 23, 43

intervention specialists 27

mental illness 32, 34–35
metal detectors 9, 25, 28–29

news 11, 19, 21, 33, 39

peacebuilders 29, 31

peer educators 27
police 9–11, 19, 25, 29, 31, 36–37, 39, 42
psychiatrists 39
psychologists 32, 39, 45

safety drills 25
Sandy Hook Elementary School 9, 18–20,
   25–26, 29, 35, 43
school violence worldwide 23
security 24–25, 28–29
social workers 39

talking 33, 37, 39
teachers 9–12, 21, 25, 27, 31, 37, 39
Teens on Target 27
therapy 19

urban schools 23
United States 11, 19, 21, 23, 26, 43

victims 14, 19, 37
video games 15, 21

witness 16, 19
witnesses 19, 37

Youth Alive! 27
Youth Justice Coalition 26–27, 29, 31
youth violence 19

About the
Author & Consultant

Kim Etingoff lives in Boston, Massachusetts. She spends part of her time working on farms, and enjoys writing on topics related to health and nutrition.

Dr. Ronald D. Stephens currently serves as executive director of the National School Safety Center. His past experience includes service as a teacher, assistant superintendent, and school board member. Administrative experience includes serving as a chief school business officer, with responsibilities over school safety and security, and as vice president of Pepperdine University.

Dr. Stephens has conducted more than 1000 school security and safety site assessments throughout the United States. He was described by the *Denver Post* as "the nation's leading school crime prevention expert." Dr. Stephens serves as consultant and frequent speaker for school districts, law enforcement agencies and professional organizations worldwide. He is the author of numerous articles on school safety as well as the author of *School Safety: A Handbook for Violence Prevention*. His career is distinguished by military service. He is married and has three children.

Picture Credits